Bible Crosswords

for Children who love God's Book

Alison Brown

KDP ISBN -9781697368208
***

Details of other titles can be found at:
www.alisonbrown.info
or
Instagram: alisonbrown.books

***

Dedicated with love
to my daughter Debbie
who still enjoys a puzzle
with her cornflakes.

Bible Words beginning with A

ACROSS
2. Brother of Moses.
4. A place of safety.
5. A stone table on which sacrifices were offered.
8. The very first man.
10. Hard-working insect found in Proverbs 6:6-8
11. Husband of Sapphira. (Acts 5:1)

DOWN
1. Father of Isaac.
3. Son of Adam.
6. A very evil king. (1 Kings 16:33)
7. Old lady who was joyful to see baby Jesus in the temple. (Luke 2:36-38)
9. Fifth book in the New Testament.

3

Bible Words beginning with B

ACROSS

5. The usual occupation of blind Bartimaeus.
6. David, the shepherd boy, carried five smooth stones in it.
7. Animal found in Leviticus 11:19
8. Brother of Joseph and a tribe of Israel. (Gen. 42:4)
9. The Hebrews, in slavery, made lots of these!

DOWN

1. Birth place of Jesus.
2. His donkey spoke to him! (Numbers 22:28)
3. Moses saw it burning in the desert. (Exod. 3)
4. Paul escaped from Damascus in it. (Acts 9:25)
7. Jesus had none of these broken when he was on the cross.

Bible Words beginning with C

ACROSS

2. Peter wept when he heard this bird crow.
4. Golden idol made by the impatient Hebrews. (Exodus 32:1-4)
5. Four legged vehicle used by many Bible people!
7. He killed his own brother.
9. Brook where Elijah was fed by the ravens. (1 Kings 17:1-3)

DOWN

1. The Israelites were led by it during the day. (Exodus 13:21)
3. The promised land.
4. Younger son of Naomi. (Ruth 1:2)
6. One of the spies, and a friend of Joshua.
8. Joseph's special coloured garment.

Bible Words beginning with D

ACROSS

2. Wise female judge and leader of Israel. (Judges 4:4)
5. King in Daniel's day. (Dan. 6)
6. One of the tribes of Israel. (Genesis 49:16)
7. The daughter of Herodius loved doing this. (Matt. 14:6)
8. The wages or punishment for sin. (Romans 6:23)

DOWN

1. God's name for light at Creation.
2. Paul met with God on this road. (Acts 9:3)
3. Only Adam was made from it. (Genesis 2:7)
4. Balaam rode one.
6. Daughter of Jacob. (Genesis 34:1)

Bible Words beginning with E

ACROSS

1. The first garden.
3. Samson lost both of his. (Judges 16:21)
5. A mighty prophet.
6. Brother of Jacob, who loved to go out hunting.
9. Lasting forever.
10. The brave Queen who was ready to die for her people.

DOWN

1. Wife of Adam.
2. Mother of John the Baptist. (Luke 1:5)
4. God made it in just six days.
6. The escape out of bondage in Egypt, led by Moses.
7. Father of Methuselah. (Genesis 5:21)
8. The old priest who trained Samuel.

Bible Words beginning with F

ACROSS

3. Where the stone hit Goliath.
4. God sent this down on Elijah's sacrifice.
5. Gideon left it out at night. (Judges 6:38)
6. Mary anointed this part of Jesus with oil. (John 12:3)
7. They were even in Pharaoh's bed! (Exodus 8:3)

DOWN

1. Rahab hid two spies under it. (Josh. 2:6)
2. Joseph said it would last for seven years.
3. Belshazzer saw them writing on the wall. (Daniel 5:5)
5. James and John used to catch them.
6. Jesus found none of these growing on the tree. (Matthew 21:19)

Bible Words beginning with G

ACROSS

4. Place where Jesus was crucified.
6. Colour of the fields Lot chose.
7. Son of Jacob and tribe of Israel. (Genesis 30:11)
8. His soldiers once fought using jars, trumpets and torches. (Judges 7)

DOWN

1. To gather leftover grain, as Ruth did.
2. Animal often used as a sin offering.
3. Lake where Jesus calmed a storm.
4. Giant who was killed by David.
5. First book in the Bible.
6. Lazarus lay in it for four days.

Bible Words beginning with H

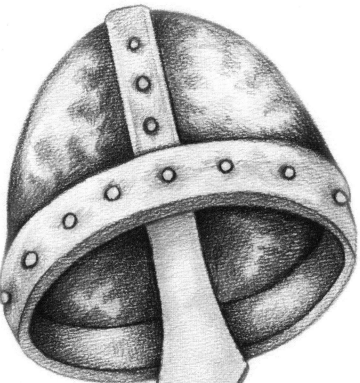

ACROSS

2. Goliath wore one, made of brass.
4. Book found in the Old Testament.
6. He was hanged on his own gallows. (Esther 7:10)
7. David's musical instrument.
8. Esau's occupation. (Genesis 25:27)

DOWN

1. King who was angry when he heard of the birth of Jesus.
2. Mother of Samuel. (1 Samuel 1:20)
3. Sarah's Egyptian maid. (Genesis 16:1)
5. Son of Noah.
7. Samson vowed he would never cut it.

Bible Words beginning with I

ACROSS

1. Bethlehem building which was full up!
3. Material used in making of King Solomon's throne. (1 Kings 10:18)
6. Father of Esau.
8. Son of Hagar. (Genesis 16:15)

DOWN

1. Paul used lots of this when writing his epistles.
2. Metal skilfully used, even before the days of Noah. (Genesis 4:22)
3. Surname of the disciple who betrayed Jesus.
4. New name given to Jacob by God. (Genesis 32:28)
5. False, man-made gods.
7. Old Testament prophet.

Bible Words beginning with J

ACROSS
2. A very evil queen.
3. When Joshua's army marched around this city its walls collapsed!
5. Brother of John. (Mark 1:19)
7. Son of Zacharias and Elisabeth. (Luke 1:5-13)
8. He tricked his elderly father using goat skins.
9. Brother of Joseph and a tribe of Israel. (Gen. 49:8)

DOWN
1. Someone who was not a Gentile.
2. The prophet who was imprisoned in a dry well. (Jer. 38:6)
4. He was swallowed by a great big fish.
6. The seven year old boy who was crowned king. (2 Kings 11:2)

More Bible Words beginning with J

ACROSS

1. Father of David.
6. She killed Sisera with a tent peg. (Judges 4:21)
7. Second last book of the Bible.
8. The man who lost all but continued to praise God!
9. King Saul threw one at David. (1 Samuel 18:11)
10. Leader of Israel after Moses. (Deut. 31:7)

DOWN

1. Jesus raised this man's daughter back to life.
2. Bible book between Hosea and Amos.
4. Samson killed one thousand Philistines with this part of an ass! (Judges 15:15)
5. One of the names we use for God. (Psalm 83:18)

Bible Words beginning with L

ACROSS

3. The blood of this animal was shed at the passover.
5. Lady who sold purple cloth. (Acts 16:14)
8. Elijah wore a girdle, or belt, made of it. (2 Kings 1:8)
9. Book in the New Testament.

DOWN

1. Jacob dreamed about one reaching up to heaven.
2. Nephew of Abraham.
4. Brother of Mary and Martha. (John 11:1-2)
5. They didn't eat Daniel!
6. Paul wrote one to the Galatians.
7. Person called 'unclean' due to a skin disease.

More Bible Words beginning with L

ACROSS

2. Rachel's sister.
3. Each wise and foolish virgins carried one.
4. A son of Jacob. (Genesis 35:23)
5. A word to describe Mephibosheth. (2 Samuel 4:4)
8. John the Baptist ate them with wild honey. (Matthew 3:1-4)
9. It caused bread dough to rise. (Luke 13:21)

DOWN

1. Brother of Rebekah and father of Rachel. (Genesis 24:29)
2. Third book in the Bible.
6. Grandmother of Timothy. (2 Tim. 1:5)
7. Something God has for all the world, and wants us to have for him! (John 3:16)

Bible Words beginning with M

DOWN

1. Oldest man in the Bible.
2. Mother of the Lord Jesus.
4. Only God can perform one of these.
6. Zacchaeus had lots of it!

ACROSS

1. Bed for baby Jesus.
3. He used to be a tax-collector. (Matt. 9:9)
5. Little girl who told Naaman about God. (2 Kings 5:2)
6. Baby hidden in a bulrush basket.
7. Book in the New Testament.
8. Son of Naomi. (Ruth 1:2)

More Bible Words beginning with M

ACROSS

3. Son of Joseph. (Genesis 41:51)
4. The disciples' name for Jesus.
6. It was created on the fourth day.
7. Bread sent down from heaven.
8. Male cousin of Queen Esther. (Esther 2:5)

DOWN

1. The name Naomi wanted to be called. (Ruth 1:20)
2. The very busy sister of Mary.
5. Country in which Ruth was born. (Ruth 1:4)
6. Father of Samson. (Judges 13:2)
7. A gift brought to baby Jesus. (Matt. 2:11)

Bible Words beginning with N

ACROSS
2. Time when the pillar of fire was seen by the Hebrews.
4. First husband of Abigail. (1 Samuel 25:3)
5. Peter fished with these.
7. The builder of the Ark.
8. The kind of ropes Delilah used to tie Samson.
9. Mother-in-law of Ruth.
10. Prophet in King David's day. (2 Samuel 7:2)

DOWN
1. The city Jonah didn't want to preach in. (Jonah 1:2)
3. Despised town in which Jesus grew up. (Luke 4:16)
6. King Ahab wanted this man's vineyard. (1 kings 21:1)

More Bible Words beginning with N

ACROSS

5. King who asked Daniel to explain the meaning of his dream. (Daniel 2)
8. Jewish ruler who went to visit Jesus by night.

DOWN

1. He led the rebuilding of Jerusalem's walls.
2. Fourth book in the Bible.
3. Sixth son of Jacob. (Genesis 30:8)
4. Bible book between Micah and Habakkuk.
6. They were used during a Roman crucifixion.
7. River in Egypt which turned red. (Exod. 7:20)

Bible Words beginning with O

ACROSS
2. Daughter-in-law of Naomi. (Ruth 1:14)
3. Working animals.
4. Ruth's baby son. (Ruth 4:17)
5. Leaf brought to Noah by the dove.
6. A promise that was never to be broken. (Genesis 26:28)

DOWN
1. Doing what God tells us to do.
2. Runaway slave, led to Christ by Paul. (Philemon 1:10)
4. Samuel used it when he anointed Saul.
5. A word to describe Methuselah.
6. Absalom was caught in its branches.

Bible Words Beginning with P

ACROSS

1. He saw a blinding light on the road to Damascus.
3. A man who gave the people special messages from God.
4. He walked on the water to Jesus!
6. Important feast in the Jewish calendar.
7. Place where Joseph met a butler and a baker. (Gen. 39:20)

DOWN

1. Type of animal fed by the hungry prodigal son.
2. King of Egypt.
3. Joseph's master while in Egypt. (Genesis 37:36)
4. A prayerful song.
5. Colour of the robe the soldiers put on Jesus.

More Bible Words beginning with P

ACROSS

1. Affliction sent from God, on the Egyptians. (Exodus 11:1)
4. Wife of Aquila. (Acts 18:2)
5. One of the twelve disciples.
8. Story told to help explain Bible truth.

DOWN

1. Goliath was one.
2. Type of branches waved to welcome Jesus.
3. Strict teachers of the Jewish Law.
5. Man who served God daily in the temple.
6. When Samson pushed it over the whole building collapsed!
7. To talk with God.

Bible Words beginning with R

ACROSS

1. Wife of Isaac. (Genesis 24:67)
2. Type of bird sent by God to feed Elijah. (1 Kings 17:6)
3. She married Boaz.
6. Promise in the sky!
8. Girl who opened the door to Peter. (Acts 12:13)
9. Noah saw lots of it!

DOWN

1. The last book in the Bible.
4. God made water flow out of it. (Exodus 17:6)
5. Jacob's eldest son. (Genesis 35:23)
7. Abraham found one caught by its horns in a thicket. (Genesis 22:13)

23

Bible Words beginning with S

ACROSS

1. Son of Noah. (Genesis 5:32)
3. It was used to pierce Jesus on the cross. (John 19:34)
4. He loved Delilah.
7. The first king of Israel. (1 Sam. 11:15)
8. Wife of Abraham.

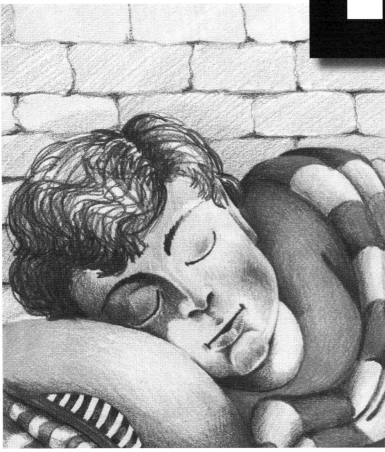

DOWN

1. Building in which the Jews worshipped.
2. Boy who heard God's voice in the darkness.
3. Something that will always separate us from God.
5. Day set apart by Jews for worshipping God.
6. Usual footwear worn in Israel.

More Bible Words beginning with S

ACROSS
1. A keeper of sheep.
2. His other name was Peter.
4. Jonah tried to escape in one.
5. It spoke to Eve in the garden.
7. Peter saw a vision of it filled with many unclean animals. (Acts 10:11)

DOWN
1. Region where Jesus met the woman at the well. (John 4:4)
3. Number of Creation days.
4. He was stoned to death by some angry Jews.
5. The wise men followed it to Bethlehem.
6. Some fell among thorns or by the wayside!

Further Bible Words beginning with S

DOWN

1. To shed the blood of an animal as an offering for sin.
2. David's weapon against the giant Goliath.
4. Evangelist who worked with the apostle Paul. (Acts 16:25)
5. Sinful city where Lot lived.
6. Mountain on which God gave the commandments to Moses. (Exodus 19:20)
7. Third son of Adam. (Gen. 4:25)

ACROSS

3. Rough cloth worn by a very sad person. (Genesis 37:34)
5. Only foolish men would build on this.
7. Jacob gave a colourful coat to his favourite one.
8. Tree climbed by Zacchaeus.

Bible Words beginning with T

ACROSS

1. Building where God was worshipped.
3. They were woven into a crown for Jesus.
4. Number of commandments.
5. Burial place used for rich people.
6. Number of days Jonah spent inside the fish.
7. Paul's home town. (Acts 21:39)

DOWN

1. The disciple who doubted that Jesus had risen again. (John 20:24-25)
2. Abraham lived in one while travelling.
3. The age of Jairus' daughter. (Luke 8:42)
4. Gideon's men blew them to frighten the enemy!

More Bible Words beginning with T

ACROSS

1. Number of silver pieces paid to Judas.
4. A very large one was built at Babel.
5. Jesus said each one would be known by its fruit. (Matt. 12:33)
7. Jesus overthrew them in the temple.
8. Many were heard at Pentecost. (Acts 2:4)
9. Number of virgins carrying oil-lamps.

DOWN

1. Earliest temple, in the desert, made of animal skins. (Exodus 33:7)
2. Bible book which comes after Timothy.
3. Number of times Daniel prayed daily.
6. Dishonest kind of man crucified next to Jesus.

Bible Words beginning with W

ACROSS

3. Rahab hung a red cord from it.
4. She fed Elijah at Zarephath. (1 Kings 17:9)
6. Abraham sent his servant to choose one for Isaac.
7. Zacharias had to do some when he couldn't speak!
9. They all fell down at Jericho.

DOWN

1. Jesus spent forty days and forty nights there.
2. The kind of man who builds on rock.
5. It flowed out when Moses struck a rock.
6. Jesus worked a miracle to provide some at a wedding. (John 2:3)
8. Jacob met his wife beside it. (Gen. 29:10)

ANSWERS

BIBLE WORDS BEGINNING WITH A
ACROSS: 2 Aaron, 4 ark, 5 altar, 8 Adam, 10 ant, 11 Ananias
DOWN: 1 Abraham, 3 Abel, 6 Ahab, 7 Anna, 9 Acts

BIBLE WORDS BEGINNING WITH B
ACROSS: 5 beggar, 6 bag, 7 bat, 8 Benjamin, 9 bricks
DOWN: 1 Bethlehem, 2 Balaam, 3 bush, 4 basket, 7 bones

BIBLE WORDS BEGINNING WITH C
ACROSS: 2 cock, 4 calf, 5 camel, 7 Cain, 9 Cherith
DOWN: 1 cloud, 3 Canaan, 4 Chilion, 6 Caleb, 8 coat

BIBLE WORDS BEGINNING WITH D
ACROSS: 2 Deborah, 5 Darius, 6 Dan, 7 dance, 8 death
DOWN: 1 day, 2 Damascus, 3 dust, 4 donkey, 6 Dinah

BIBLE WORDS BEGINNING WITH E
ACROSS: 1 Eden, 3 eyes, 5 Elijah (or Elisha), 6 Esau, 9 eternal, 10 Esther
DOWN: 1 Eve, 2 Elisabeth, 4 Earth, 6 Exodus, 7 Enoch, 8 Eli

BIBLE WORD BEGINNING WITH F
ACROSS: 3 forehead, 4 fire, 5 fleece, 6 feet, 7 frogs
DOWN: 1 flax, 2 famine, 3 fingers, 5 fish, 6 figs

BIBLE WORDS BEGINNING WITH G
ACROSS: 4 Golgotha, 6 green, 7 Gad, 8 Gideon
DOWN: 1 glean, 2 goat, 3 Galilee, 4 Goliath, 5 Genesis, 6 grave

BIBLE WORD BEGINNING WITH H
ACROSS: 2 helmet, 4 Hosea, 6 Haman, 7 harp, 8 hunter
DOWN: 1 Herod, 2 Hannah, 3 Hagar, 5 Ham, 7 hair

BIBLE WORDS BEGINNING WITH I
ACROSS: 1 inn, 3 ivory, 6 Isaac, 8 Ishmael
DOWN: 1 ink, 2 iron, 3 Iscariot, 4 Israel, 5 idols, 7 Isaiah

BIBLE WORDS BEGINNING WITH J
ACROSS: 2 Jezebel, 3 Jericho, 5 James, 7 John, 8 Jacob, 9 Judah
DOWN: 1 Jew, 2 Jeremiah, 4 Jonah, 6 Joash

MORE BIBLE WORDS BEGINNING WITH J
ACROSS: 1 Jesse, 6 Jael, 7 Jude, 8 Job, 9 Javelin, 10 Joshua
DOWN: 1 Jairus, 2 Joel, 4 Jawbone, 5 Jehovah

BIBLE WORDS BEGINNING WITH L
ACROSS: 3 lamb, 5 Lydia, 8 leather, 9 Luke
DOWN: 1 ladder, 2 Lot, 4 Lazarus, 5 lions, 6 letter, 7 leper

MORE BIBLE WORDS BEGINNING WITH L
ACROSS: 2 Leah, 3 lamp, 4 Levi, 5 lame 8 locusts, 9 leaven
DOWN: 1 Laban, 2 Leviticus, 6 Lois, 7 Love

BIBLE WORDS BEGINNING WITH M
ACROSS: 1 manger, 3 Matthew, 5 maid, 6 Moses, 7 Mark, 8 Mahlon
DOWN: 1 Methuselah, 2 Mary, 4 miracle, 6 money

MORE BIBLE WORDS BEGINNING WITH M
ACROSS: 3 Manasseh, 4 Master, 6 moon, 7 manna, 8 Mordecai,
DOWN: 1 Mara, 2 Martha, 5 Moab, 6 Manoah, 7 myrrh

BIBLE WORDS BEGINNING WITH N
ACROSS: 2 night, 4 Nabal, 5 nets, 7 Noah, 8 new, 9 Naomi, 10 Nathan
DOWN: 1 Nineveh, 3 Nazareth, 6 Naboth

MORE BIBLE WORDS BEGINNING WITH N
ACROSS: 5 Nebuchadnezzar, 8 Nicodemus
DOWN: 1 Nehemiah, 2 Numbers, 3 Naphtali, 4 Nahum, 6 nails, 7 Nile

BIBLE WORDS BEGINNING WITH O
ACROSS: 2. Orpah, 3 oxen, 4 Obed, 5 olive, 6 oath
DOWN: 1 obedience, 2 Onesimus, 4 oil, 5 old, 6 oak

BIBLE WORDS BEGINNING WITH P
ACROSS: 1 Paul, 3 prophet, 4 Peter, 6 Passover, 7 prison
DOWN: 1 pig, 2 Pharaoh, 3 Potiphar, 4 psalm, 5 purple

MORE BIBLE WORDS BEGINNING WITH P

ACROSS: 1 plague, 4 Priscilla, 5 Philip, 8 parable
DOWN: 1 Philistine, 2 palm, 3 Pharisees, 5 priest, 6 pillar, 7 pray

BIBLE WORDS BEGINNING WITH R

ACROSS: 1 Rebekah, 2 raven, 3 Ruth, 6 rainbow, 8 Rhoda, 9 rain
DOWN: 1 Revelation, 4 rock, 5 Reuben, 7 ram

BIBLE WORDS BEGINNING WITH S

ACROSS: 1 Shem, 3 spear, 4 Samson, 7 Saul, 8 Sarah
DOWN: 1 synagogue, 2 Samuel, 3 sin, 5 sabbath, 6 sandal

MORE BIBLE WORDS BEGINNING WITH S

ACROSS: 1 shepherd, 2 Simon, 4 ship, 5 serpent, 7 sheet
DOWN: 1 Samaria, 3 six, 4 Stephen, 5 star, 6 seed

FURTHER BIBLE WORDS BEGINNING S

ACROSS: 3 sackcloth, 5 sand, 7 son, 8 sycamore
DOWN: 1 sacrifice, 2 sling, 4 Silas, 5 Sodom, 6 Sinai, 7 Seth

BIBLE WORDS BEGINNING WITH T

ACROSS: 1 temple, 3 thorns, 4 ten, 5 tomb, 6 three, 7 Tarsus
DOWN: 1 Thomas, 2 tent, 3 twelve, 4 trumpets

MORE BIBLE WORDS BEGINNING WITH T

ACROSS: 1 thirty, 4 tower, 5 tree, 7 tables, 8 tongues, 9 ten
DOWN: 1 tabernacle, 2 Titus, 3 three, 6 thief

BIBLE WORDS BEGINNING WITH W

ACROSS: 3 window, 4 widow, 6 wife, 7 writing, 9 walls
DOWN: 1 wilderness, 2 wise, 5 water, 6 wine, 8 well

Printed in Poland
by Amazon Fulfillment
Poland Sp. z o.o., Wrocław

56949345R00020

SCIENCE WORKS

SUN UP, SUN DOWN

THE STORY OF DAY AND NIGHT

FALKIRK COUNCIL
LIBRARY SUPPORT
FOR SCHOOLS

OH, GOOD... A BEDTIME STORY.

Jacqui Bailey   Matthew Lilly

A & C BLACK • LONDON

The night sky was pitch black and the garden was dark. It was long after midnight and everything was quiet.

Most animals were fast asleep, curled up in holes and burrows and nests.

The family was fast asleep too. A porch light shone, but the rest of the house was closed and still.

4

Then a breeze rustled the leaves of a tree. Behind the house, a strip of light appeared between the land and the sky.

The light grew stronger and brighter. It pushed back the dark and the sky changed from black to grey to blue.

Streaks of sunlight raced over the land and the Sun bulged into view.

It was dawn — time to start another day.

Bit by bit the Sun rose in the sky, sending out its beams of light, called rays.

When the rays hit the garden they started warming everything up.

The damp grass steamed as it began to dry — and life suddenly got busier.

MMM!

SLURP!

Plants lifted up their leaves and greedily soaked up the Sun's rays. It had been a long, dark night and they needed the energy in the sunlight to make their food.

Insects uncurled and crawled into the sunshine. Other animals stretched and yawned. They were hungry too.

MMM, BREAKFAST!

MMM, BREAKFAST!

OOOH, THAT'S BETTER. NOTHING LIKE A BIT OF SUNLIGHT TO START THE DAY.

Some chomped on plants . . . some gobbled up insects . . .

MMM, BREAKFAST!

. . . and some ate just about anything they could get their hands on!

The Sun's light and heat shine so strongly on us, you might think it was close by. But it's not. It's millions and millions of kilometres away.

The reason we can see and feel it from so far away is because the Sun itself is incredibly bright and hot. So hot, that it's impossible to get anywhere near it. Scientists can take photographs of it, though . . .

RUMBLE!
RUMBLE!
BOOM!
BOOM!

RUMBLE!
RUMBLE!
BOOM!

. . . and they've discovered that the Sun is a gigantic ball of superhot gases. Deep inside it, billions of explosions are taking place every second, and it is these explosions that create all that raging heat and light.

The Sun was giving out other types of rays, too!

Some of the Sun's other rays, such as x-rays and ultraviolet rays, can be harmful to life on Earth.

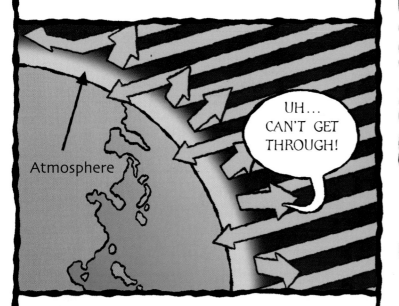

Luckily, many of them are blocked out by Earth's atmosphere — this is the band of gases that covers the Earth — but some do get through.

So the children covered themselves in sun lotion to help block out any harmful rays that might damage their skin.

With the Sun high overhead, it was hard to find anywhere shady and cool in the garden.

The children put up a big umbrella and sat in the shadow beneath it.

Light rays can pass through some materials — the same ones you can see through, such as glass and clear plastic.

But things you can't see through, like wood or stone, block out light rays and a shadow appears on the other side of them.

All kinds of things make shadows on sunny days — houses, trees, fences, flower pots, even you! But shadows are always changing.

1 In the morning, when the Sun is low down in the sky, the shadows are long.

2 As the Sun climbs higher, the shadows get shorter.

3 When the Sun is at its highest, there are almost no shadows at all.

4 In the afternoon, the shadows get longer again — but this time they are on the other side!

The garden sweltered in the afternoon heat. But the Sun didn't stay high overhead.

It gradually swung across to the other side of the sky and slid towards the land.

IS IT SUPPER TIME YET?

Slowly the shadows lengthened and the sky grew darker.

I PREFER FOOD FROM A TIN.

EEEEK!

Most of the animals in the garden (and the family) got ready to go to sleep. But not all! Some liked the dark and coolness of evening — for them it was the best time to find their food.

14

The Sun sank into the ground and the last bits of sunlight glowed orange and red in the sky. Then the Sun was gone. The sky was black and it was night time again.

But, hang on a minute, the Sun hadn't really gone into the ground . . . had it?

Well, no, it hadn't. It hadn't moved across the sky at all. It just looked like it had. In fact, it was the Earth that moved — but you'd have to be in a spaceship to see it!

From a spaceship you would see the Earth as a bright, beautiful ball, hanging in the blackness of Space.

But it's not just hanging there – it's moving all the time. It's spinning around and around, just like a giant spinning top.

As the Earth spins, half of it is turned away from the Sun. The Sun's light doesn't reach it so for this side it's night time...

The spinning doesn't make us dizzy because the Earth never ever changes its speed or the direction in which it spins. And we're so used to it, we don't feel a thing!

The Earth takes 23 hours and 56 minutes to spin around once.

ALMOST 24 HOURS, THAT'S ONE WHOLE DAY!

The Earth spins at about 1,600 kilometres an hour — nearly twice as fast as a jumbo jet.

. . . but the other half of the Earth is turned towards the Sun and is lit up by it. So for this side it's daytime.

1 At dawn, when the Sun rose over the garden, this part of the Earth was just turning towards the Sun.

2 At midday, the garden was face to face with the Sun.

3 When it was evening in the garden, this part of the Earth was turning away from the Sun.

4 At midnight, the garden was facing the opposite direction to the Sun. It was in the Earth's shadow.

However . . . even though it was night time in the garden, the sky wasn't entirely black. A glowing lantern of light hung there. It was the Moon.

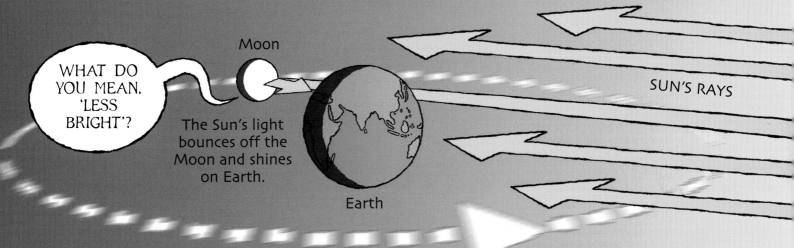

WHAT DO YOU MEAN, 'LESS BRIGHT'?

Moon

The Sun's light bounces off the Moon and shines on Earth.

Earth

SUN'S RAYS

The Moon is far less bright than the Sun. That's because it doesn't make any light of its own. It is a lifeless ball of rock. It only shines because the Sun's light is bouncing off it.

The Moon is our closest neighbour in Space, but it isn't only a neighbour. It travels around and around the Earth — just as the Earth travels around the Sun.

That's right! The Earth moves in two completely different ways. As well as spinning around on itself, it's also travelling in circles (well, sort of egg-shaped circles) around the Sun! This huge, looping journey is called an orbit.

DON'T YOU GUYS EVER GET TIRED OF DOING THE SAME OLD THING?

It takes the Earth 365.25 days to make one complete orbit of the Sun. That's one whole year.

The Moon orbits the Earth while the Earth orbits the Sun.

Earth's orbit is 958 million kilometres long, and the Earth zips around it at 108,000 kilometres per hour — that's almost four times the speed of a Space Shuttle!

The Earth never stops, or slows down. It's been orbiting the Sun for about 4 1/2 billion years, and it will keep going for billions more.

And do you know what the really amazing thing is?
Earth's orbit is exactly the right distance from the Sun!

Any closer, and the Earth would get too hot. The oceans would dry up and the world would be an empty desert.

Any further away and the Earth would get too cold. The whole world would become a huge iceball.

But the Earth is not too close, or too far away. So we have just the right amount of heat and light for plants and animals — including us — to live.

And that's nearly the end of the story . . . but not quite . . . because the Moon wasn't the only light in the night sky. There were also hundreds, even thousands of tiny twinkling pinpricks of light. They were stars!

WOW! LOOK AT ALL THOSE STARS...

But even the stars aren't really the way they look from Earth.

Those tiny twinkling lights are billions upon billions of kilometres away, and every single one of them is a gigantic, glowing, scorchingly hot sun, like our own.

And you never know . . . maybe one of those far-away suns has a world going around it that's just like Earth. And maybe someone is sitting on that world, too, reading about their sun!

WHICH IS BIGGEST?

From Earth, the Sun and the Moon look much the same size. But the Moon is really only a quarter of the size of Earth, whereas the Sun is more than a hundred times bigger!

So if the Earth was the size of a cherry stone, then the Sun would be as big as a beachball, and the Moon would be almost as small as a pinhead!

I'M SCARED!

HOW FAR?

ZOOOMMM!

PUFF! PANT!

The Sun is 150 million kilometres from Earth. If you climbed in a car and drove there at 100 kilometres per hour, it would take you about 171 years to arrive. Although the heat from the Sun would have fried you to a crisp long before you got there!

But sunlight travels much faster. It takes just over 8 minutes for a ray of sunlight to get from the Sun to the surface of the Earth.

MOVING AROUND

No matter where you live on Earth, the Sun always rises more or less in the east and sets more or less in the west.

Exactly where you see the Sun rise or set depends on what time of year it is. In winter the Sun is lower in the sky than in summer, even at midday. And it rises later and sets earlier.

Midday is the half-way point between rising and setting, when the Sun is at its highest in the sky. We say that midday is at 12 o'clock, but the Sun doesn't always reach its highest point at exactly this time.

GIANTS AND DWARFS

Even stars don't last forever. One day, about 5 billion years from now, our Sun will start to go out.

To begin with it will swell up — growing as much as 100 times bigger. It will become what scientists call a 'red giant'. Hopefully, by this time we'll have moved somewhere else, as Earth will be baked to a cinder.

Then the Sun will start to shrink. Over millions more years it will turn into a small white star about the size of Earth. Scientists call this a 'white dwarf'. After this, our Sun will slowly fade away.

Midday in summer

Midday in winter

Sunrise

Sunset

Red Giant

White Dwarf

TRY IT AND SEE

SUN TIME

Thousands of years ago, before we invented clocks and watches, people used the Sun to help them measure time. They did it by making something called a sundial.

OH GOOD, IT'S TIME FOR TEA.

Have a go at making your own sundial. It will take the best part of a day, so choose a time when you don't have to be anywhere special — and when the Sun is shining!

You will need:
- A large sheet of white card or paper
- Some plasticine or play dough
- A wooden stick, such as a pencil
- A felt-tip pen and a ruler
- An alarm clock

1 Choose a good spot to make your sundial. It needs to be outside in the open where no shadows will fall on it as the day goes by — and where it won't be moved.

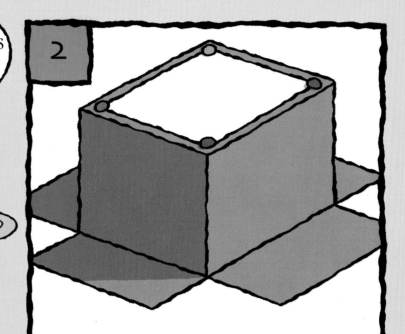

2 Put the sheet of paper or card on a firm, flat surface — such as a table, a paving stone, or even an upturned tray or cardboard box.

If you are using paper, put a stone on each corner to hold the paper in place.

3   Use the plasticine to make a base for the wooden stick. Make sure the stick will stand upright. Then place the stick and the base in the middle of your paper. Draw a circle around the base to mark its position and don't move it.

    The stick is called the gnomon (*no-mon*). When the Sun shines on it, the gnomon will make a shadow on the paper.

4   Start as early as you can in the morning. Set your alarm clock to go off every hour during the day so you don't forget. Each time the alarm goes off, check the position of the shadow on the paper and draw a line along it with the felt-tip and ruler.

Keep your sundial in place and the next day you can use it to find out what the time is without looking at a clock. As long as the Sun is shining, of course!

27

SHINING FACTS

The Sun's light may only take about 8 minutes to get to the Earth, but the energy that creates it takes over a million years to get from the centre of the Sun to its surface.

BRIGHT... YET VERY SLOW.

THIS COULD TAKE SOME TIME.

The distance from one star to another is so vast that scientists measure distance in Space in 'light-years'. One light-year is the distance travelled by a light ray in one year — which is 9,500 billion kilometres!

The surface of the Sun seems smooth from a distance, but it is always bubbling with energy. Every now and then, huge flares of hot gas spurt out into Space. They can stretch for thousands of kilometres before falling back to the Sun.

INDEX

SOME SUNNY WEBSITES TO VISIT

http://amazing-space.stsci.edu = Amazing Space: Education On-Line from the Hubble Space Telescope. A brilliant site with loads of activities all about Space.

http://starchild.gsfc.nasa.gov = StarChild: 'A Learning Center for Young Astronomers', created by NASA's High Energy Astrophysics Science Archive Research Center, which is a very complicated name for such a fun site!

http://observe.arc.nasa.gov = NASA's Observatorium. Go to the 'Gallery' for fabulous photos of views of the Earth and Space.

For Vickie
JB

For Oliver, Timothy and Gregory
ML

First published in 2003 by
A & C Black Publishers Limited
37 Soho Square, London W1D 3QZ
www.acblack.com

Created for A & C Black Publishers Limited by
two's COMPANY
Copyright © Two's Company 2003

ISBN 0 7136 6253 0 (hbk)
ISBN 0 7136 6254 9 (pbk)

Printed in Hong Kong by Wing King Tong

A & C Black uses paper produced with elemental chlorine-free
pulp, harvested from managed sustainable forests.